15 HABITS OF A HAPPY HUSBAND

15 HABITS OF A HAPPY HUSBAND

A guide to cultivating joy, intimacy, and spiritual strength in marriage

DAVID SCOTT, ED.D., D.MIN.

PCB

Published by Purple Chair Books and Educational Products, LLC

First Printing, 2025

Scott, David 1969-

15 Habits of a Happy Husband

By David Scott

ISBN: 978-1-953671-12-7

Self-Help/Inspirational

Printed in the United States of America

Interior designed by Md Al Amin (aminbookdesign@gmail.com)

Cover designed by Sadia A @sadia_coverz

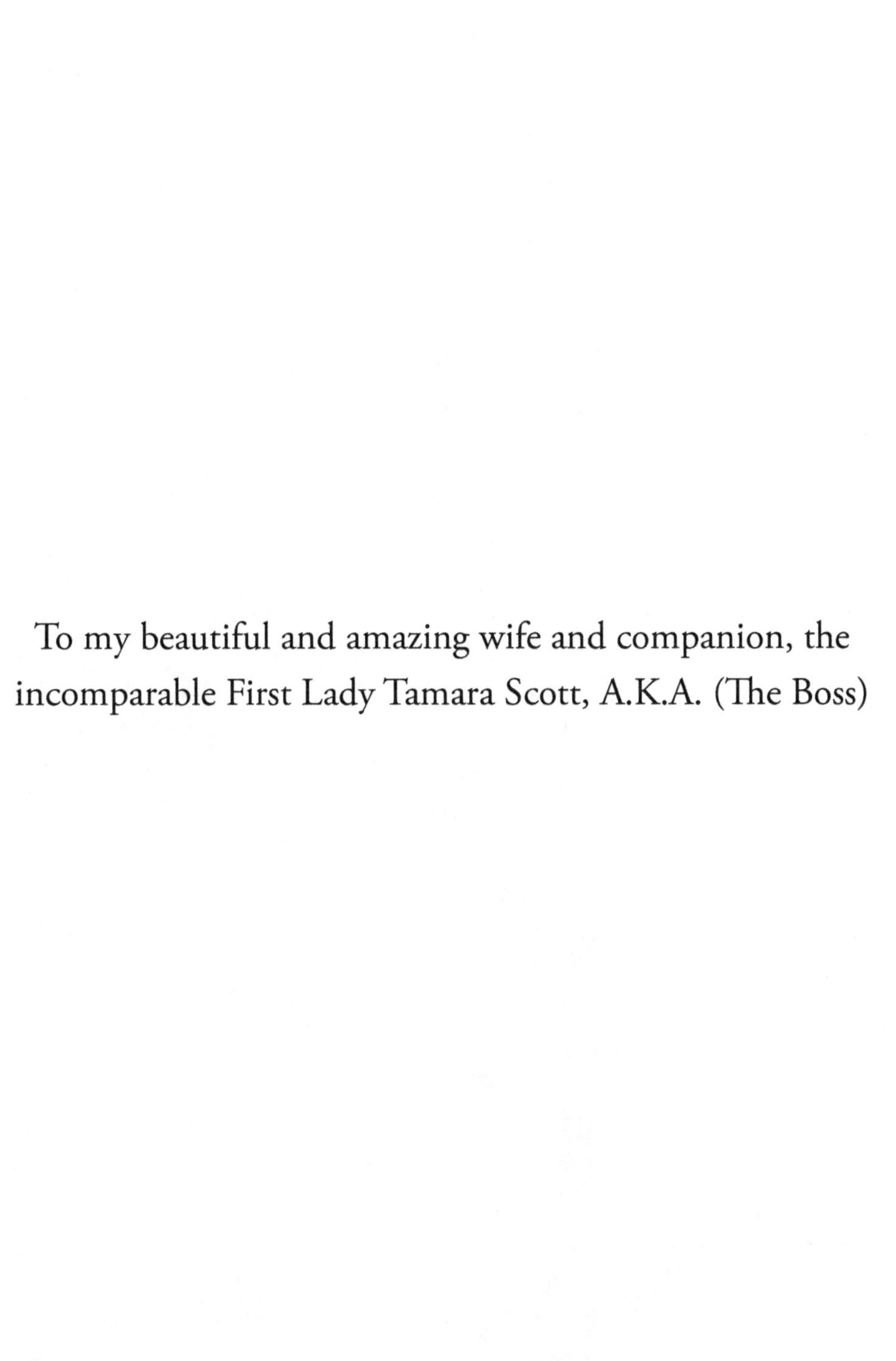

To my beautiful and amazing wife and companion, the incomparable First Lady Tamara Scott, A.K.A. (The Boss)

Foreword

By someone who's walked the road and still believes in the beauty of the vow…

There's something sacred about a man who chooses to love well. Not just once at the altar, but every day—in the quiet moments, the hard conversations, the everyday routines. A man who doesn't settle for merely surviving marriage but aims to thrive in it. A man who views his role not as a burden, but as a calling. That kind of husband is rare. But he's not mythical. He's made—not born. And he's shaped through habits.

15 Habits of a Happy Husband is more than a book. On the contrary, it is a mirror, a map, and a mentor. It reflects the man you are, guides you toward who you're becoming, and speaks with the voice of a mentor who's not here to shame you but to refine you.

This book avoids clichés and shallow sentiment. It is rooted in truth, shaped by experience, and filled with grace. It doesn't ask you to be perfect. It asks you to be present. It doesn't require performance. It encourages transformation.

Every habit in these pages is a doorway to more profound joy, richer intimacy, and stronger spiritual leadership. Whether you're a newlywed learning the rhythm of love, a seasoned husband navigating life's complexities, or a man seeking restoration after brokenness—this book meets you where you are and walks with you toward where you could be.

I've seen marriages revived through the power of humility. I've watched husbands rediscover laughter, rebuild trust, and reignite passion—not with grand gestures, but through everyday faithfulness. That's what this book provides: a guide for becoming the kind of man who brings life to his home, strength to his wife, and legacy to his children.

Take your time with it. Read it prayerfully. Read it with a pen in hand and an open heart. And as you do, remember this: happiness in marriage isn't discovered—it's built. And you, dear brother, have everything you need to start.

Let the habits start. Let the joy come back. *Let the husband get up*!

Table of Contents

Introduction

The Joy of Being a Husband

Why happiness in marriage is not accidental—and how habits shape the man behind the vow.

There's a quiet ache in the hearts of many husbands. Not because they don't love their wives, but because somewhere along the way, joy has been buried beneath the weight of responsibility, routine, or regret. The honeymoon has faded. The calendar is full. The laughter has thinned. And now, in the silence between dinner and bedtime, a question lingers: Is this all there is?

Let me tell you—no, it's not.

Marriage was never intended to drift into emotional distance or spiritual exhaustion gradually. It was created by God to be a covenant of joy, a partnership of purpose, and a daily call to love like Christ. But joy doesn't just happen. It's not a stroke of luck or a personality skill. It's built through habits.

This book isn't about quick fixes or superficial advice. It's a guide for husbands who want to go beyond being just good providers or passive partners. It's for men who want to fully live in their marriages—spiritually engaged, emotionally available, and relationally connected. It's for husbands who see happiness as sacred and love as an active verb.

Each chapter discusses a habit that, when practiced consistently, can transform not only your marriage but also your soul. These habits are grounded in Scripture, guided by wisdom, and tested through real-life experiences. They are not about achieving perfection; they are about pursuit. The pursuit of becoming the man your wife can trust, laugh with, lean on, and grow old beside.

You don't have to be a theologian, a romantic, or a perfect communicator to start. You need to be willing—willing to pray, willing to listen, willing to grow, and willing to love with intention.

Whether you're newly married or have decades together, whether your marriage is thriving or barely holding on, this book is for you. It's not about fixing her—it's about shaping you. Because when a husband becomes whole, the marriage begins to heal. And when a husband becomes happy—not in a shallow, self-centered way, but in a deep, Christ-centered way—his joy becomes contagious.

Let's start not with guilt, but with grace, not with pressure, but with promise. You were made for this, and your wife deserves the best version of you—not someday but starting now.

Let's develop the habits that bring happiness to a husband. And let's rediscover the joy that God originally intended.

PART I:
HABITS OF THE HEART

CHAPTER ONE

He Prays Daily–for Her and with Her

Prayer is the heartbeat of a spiritually connected marriage. This chapter explores how husbands can intercede for their wives, pray with them regularly, and cultivate a shared spiritual rhythm that deepens intimacy and invites God's presence into daily life.

The Sacred Rhythm of Intercession and Intimacy

He doesn't just pray *about* her.
He prays *for* her.
And he prays *with* her.
Daily.

This is not a ritual of obligation; it is a rhythm of love. A husband who intercedes for his wife is not merely fulfilling a spiritual duty; he is stepping into the priestly role God has entrusted to him. In the quiet moments of prayer, he becomes her spiritual covering, her advocate before the throne of grace, and her partner in divine communion.

Intercession: Standing in the Gap

To intercede is to stand between. It is to lift her name, her needs, her dreams, and her battles before the Lord—not as a distant observer, but as one who bears her burdens in love.

He prays for her emotional health, asking God to soothe her anxieties and renew her joy.

- He prays for her physical strength, believing for healing, energy, and rest.

- He prays for her spiritual growth, that she would flourish in the Word and walk boldly in her calling.
- He prays for her relationships, her work, her ministry, her motherhood, her friendships.

This kind of prayer is not passive. On the contrary, it is warfare. It is the husband wielding the sword of the Spirit on her behalf, declaring truth over lies, peace over chaos, and victory over weariness.

Spiritual Intimacy: Beyond Physical Connection

When a husband and wife pray together, something sacred unfolds. Their souls align in the presence of God. Vulnerability deepens. Walls fall. Hearts soften.

Spiritual intimacy is the deepest form of connection a couple can share. It transcends the physical and emotional—it is communion with God and with one another.

- In shared prayer, they confess and forgive.
- In shared prayer, they dream and discern.
- In shared prayers, they worship and weep.
- In shared prayer, they become one—not just in body, but in spirit.

This is the kind of intimacy that sustains a marriage through storms. It is the glue that binds when words fail and emotions fray. It is the sacred space where love is rekindled, and hope is restored.

Shared Devotion: Building a Spiritual Legacy

A husband who leads in devotion is not dominating—he is serving. He is saying, "Let's seek God together. Let's build our house on the Rock."

Whether it's five minutes in the morning or a quiet moment before bed, shared devotion creates a spiritual rhythm that shapes the atmosphere of the home.

- Reading Scripture together anchors their hearts in truth.
- Reflecting on God's promises renews their faith.

- Praying over their children, their finances, and their future invites divine direction.

This is not about perfection, but about presence. It's about showing up, day after day, with open hearts and open hands, saying, "Lord, lead us."

Practical Ways to Cultivate Daily Prayer

- **Start Small**: One verse, one prayer, one moment of gratitude.
- **Be Intentional**: Schedule it. Protect it. Prioritize it.
- **Be Honest**: Pray raw prayers. God honors authenticity.
- **Be Creative**: Use devotionals, prayer journals, worship music, or even voice memos.
- **Be Consistent**: Even when it feels dry, keep showing up. The well will fill.

A Prayer for Husbands

Lord, teach me to pray for her with tenderness and power. Make me a man of intercession, a priest in our home, a partner in her spiritual journey. Let our prayers be the altar where Your presence dwells, and our marriage the sanctuary of Your love. Amen.

"Intimacy is built in the quiet choices: listening longer, forgiving faster, and praying together more often."

Reflection

CHAPTER TWO

He Practices Gratitude

Gratitude transforms perspective. By intentionally noticing and naming the good in his wife and marriage, a husband shifts the emotional climate of the home. This chapter offers practical ways to build a habit of thankfulness—even in seasons of struggle.

Gratitude Is a Discipline—Not Just a Feeling

He doesn't wait to feel thankful.
He chooses to *practice* gratitude.
Daily. Intentionally. Audibly.

Gratitude is not a passive emotion—it's a spiritual discipline. It's the act of noticing, naming, and nurturing the good. A husband who practices gratitude is a man who refuses to let criticism, fatigue, or disappointment define the atmosphere of his home. He speaks life. He sees beauty. He remembers grace.

Gratitude is how he fights cynicism.
It's how he softens conflict.
It's how he honors his wife.

Noticing the Good: The Eyes of Grace

Gratitude begins with *noticing*. It's the decision to see what's right, not just what's wrong. It's the spiritual posture of scanning the day for evidence of God's goodness—and her goodness.

- He notices her laughter and lets it linger.
- He notices her sacrifices and names them aloud.

- He notices her beauty—not just physical, but the radiance of her character.
- He notices the small things: the way she folds towels, the way she prays, the way she keeps showing up.

This kind of noticing is holy. It's the antidote to entitlement. It's the lens of grace that sees his wife not as a problem to fix, but as a gift to cherish.

Speaking Life: Words That Build, Not Break

Gratitude must be spoken. Silent appreciation is good—but *verbal affirmation* is powerful.

- "Thank you for how you handled that."
- "I love the way you care for our family."
- "I'm grateful for your wisdom."
- "You are a blessing to me."

These words are not flattery. No, they are truth. They are seeds that grow trust, intimacy, and joy. When a husband speaks life, he creates a culture of honor. He builds emotional safety. He disarms defensiveness.

In moments of tension, gratitude can be a bridge.
In seasons of stress, it can be a balm.
In the daily grind, it can be a spark.

Journaling Thankfulness: A Legacy of Remembrance

A gratitude journal is more than a notebook—it's a spiritual archive. It's a place where he records the fingerprints of God and the fingerprints of grace in his marriage.

- He writes down answered prayers.
- He writes down moments of laughter.
- He writes down things she said that moved him.
- He writes down memories that matter.

This practice reshapes his perspective. It trains his heart to remember. It becomes a well he can draw from when the days feel dry. And one day, it may become a legacy his children read—a testimony of faithfulness and love.

Gratitude Reshapes Perspective and Softens Conflict

Gratitude doesn't ignore problems—it reframes them. It doesn't erase conflict—it softens it.

- When he's frustrated, gratitude reminds him of her heart.
- When he's tired, gratitude reminds him of her effort.
- When he's tempted to withdraw, gratitude calls him to lean in.

Gratitude is not weakness—it's strength. It's the spiritual muscle that lifts the marriage above petty grievances and into the realm of grace.

Practical Ways to Practice Gratitude in Marriage

- Start the Day with Thanks: One sentence of appreciation before coffee.
- Use Sticky Notes: Leave affirmations where she'll find them.
- Create a Gratitude Jar: Drop in daily blessings and read them together monthly.
- End the Day with Reflection: Share one thing you're thankful for before sleep.
- Write a Monthly Letter: A short note of gratitude for her heart, her growth, her love.

A Prayer for Husband

Lord, train my eyes to see the good.
Teach my tongue to speak life.
Make me a man of remembrance,
Who honors my wife with gratitude,
And builds our home with thanksgiving.
Let my words be healing,
My heart be soft,
And my spirit be full of praise.
Amen.

"The happiest husbands are students of their wives—always learning, always loving."

Reflection

CHAPTER THREE

He Chooses Forgiveness Quickly

Lingering resentment poisons joy. This chapter teaches husbands how to release offense, seek reconciliation, and model Christlike forgiveness. It includes tools for conflict resolution and stories of restoration.

Forgiveness is not weakness, it's warfare. A man who forgives quickly is a man who refuses to let bitterness take root, who fights for joy, and who models the radical grace of Christ in every relationship.

The Poison of Lingering Resentment

Resentment is a slow-burning toxin. It disguises itself as self-protection but corrodes intimacy, clarity, and peace. Lingering offense:

- Distorts how we see others and ourselves
- Fuels passive aggression and emotional withdrawal
- Blocks spiritual growth and prayer (see Matthew 6:14–15)
- Robs marriages, friendships, and ministries of vitality

Illustration:

A husband once said, "I'm not angry—I just don't care anymore." But indifference is often resentment in disguise. The longer we nurse the wound, the deeper the infection.

Christlike Forgiveness: A Bold, Immediate Choice

Jesus didn't delay forgiveness. On the cross, He said, "Father, forgive them..." while nails were still in His hands. Forgiveness is not a feeling—it's a decision to release someone from the debt they owe you.

To forgive quickly is to:

- Refuse to rehearse the offense
- Release the need for revenge or vindication
- Trust God to be the righteous Judge
- Choose love over pride

Scripture Anchor:

"Bear with each other and forgive one another if any of you has a grievance... Forgive as the Lord forgave you." —Colossians 3:13

Tools for Conflict Resolution & Reconciliation

Forgiveness is the foundation, but reconciliation is the bridge. Here are practical tools to walk it out:

1. The 24-Hour Rule

Don't let offense linger. If something hurts, address it within 24 hours—calmly, prayerfully, and respectfully.

2. The "I Feel" Framework

Instead of accusations, use statements like:
"I feel hurt when…"
"I need clarity about…"
This invites dialogue, not defensiveness.

3. Own Your Part

Even if you were 10% wrong, own it fully. Humility disarms hostility.

4. Pray Before You Speak

Ask God to soften your heart and give you words that heal, not harm.

5. Invite a Mediator

In deep conflict, a trusted pastor, counselor, or mentor can help both parties hear each other and move toward restoration.

Restoration Stories: Grace in Action

Story 1: The Silent Marriage

James and Tanya hadn't spoken kindly in months. Resentment had built a wall. One night, James read Ephesians 4:32 and felt convicted. He wrote a letter of apology, owning his harshness and asking for forgiveness. Tanya wept. That letter became the turning point toward healing.

Story 2: The Broken Brotherhood

Two ministry partners split over a financial misunderstanding. Years passed. One reached out with a simple text: "I miss you. Can we talk?" That conversation led to tears, truth-telling, and a renewed partnership—stronger than before.

Forgiveness as Legacy

A man who forgives quickly leaves a legacy of grace. His children learn how to love through conflict. His wife feels safe to be vulnerable. His church sees Christ in his humility. His enemies are disarmed by his mercy.

Challenge:

Who do you need to forgive today? What offense are you still rehearsing? Choose release. Choose reconciliation. Choose Christ.

Closing Prayer

Lord, teach me to forgive quickly.
Strip away my pride, my need to be right, my desire to punish.
Fill me with Your mercy.
Help me release offense and pursue peace.
Make me a man who models Your grace—boldly, humbly, and consistently.
In Jesus' name, Amen.

"The strongest marriages aren't conflict-free—they're grace-filled.

Reflection

CHAPTER FOUR

He Cultivates Emotional Honesty

Genuine connection requires vulnerability. This chapter helps husbands name their emotions, listen empathetically, and create a safe space for their wives to do the same. Emotional honesty becomes a bridge to deeper trust.

Emotional honesty is not weakness; it's courageous leadership. A man who names his feelings and shares them with humility becomes a safe place for intimacy, healing, and trust. In marriage, emotional honesty is the bridge between isolation and connection.

Why Emotional Honesty Matters

Many men were taught to suppress emotion, to "man up" and push through. But silence isn't strength, it's a slow erosion of intimacy. Emotional honesty:

- Builds trust and safety in marriage
- Prevents resentment and emotional withdrawal
- Models Christlike vulnerability and compassion
- Strengthens spiritual and relational maturity

Illustration:

A wife once said, "I'd rather hear my husband say he's scared than pretend he's fine." Emotional honesty doesn't diminish masculinity, it deepens it.

Naming Feelings: The First Step to Freedom

You can't heal what you won't name. Feelings are signals, not threats. Naming them helps you process, not suppress.

Common emotions men often avoid:

Fear	"I'm afraid I'll fail you."
Shame	"I feel like I'm not enough."
Anger	"I'm frustrated and I don't know what to do."
Sadness	"I feel heavy and I don't know why."
Joy	"I feel grateful for how you love me."

Tool:

Use a "Feelings Wheel" to expand your emotional vocabulary. The more precise your language, the more powerful your connection.

Sharing Vulnerably: Strength in Transparency

Vulnerability isn't dumping emotion, it's inviting connection. It says, "I trust you with the real me."

Keys to sharing vulnerably:

- Speak from your own experience, not accusations
- Use "I feel" statements, not "You always…"
- Share without demanding a fix—just presence
- Be willing to be misunderstood, and clarify gently

Scripture Anchor:

"Confess your sins to one another and pray for one another, that you may be healed."—James 5:16
Confession isn't just about sin—it's about truth-telling that leads to healing.

Listening Deeply: The Gift of Presence

Listening is more than hearing—it's honoring. Deep listening says, "You matter. Your heart matters."

Practices for deep listening:

- Maintain eye contact and open posture
- Reflect back what you hear: "So you're feeling…"
- Resist the urge to fix—just be present
- Ask clarifying questions: "Can you tell me more?"

Tool:

Practice "Active Listening" with your spouse weekly. Set aside 15 minutes where one speaks and the other listens—without interruption or correction.

Emotional Intelligence in Marriage: Tools for Growth

Emotional intelligence (EQ) is the ability to recognize, understand, and manage emotions—yours and others. It's essential for healthy conflict resolution and intimacy.

Core EQ Skills:

Skill	Marriage Application
Self-awareness	"I'm feeling triggered—let me pause."
Self-regulation	"I'll take a walk before we continue."
Empathy	"I can see why that hurt you."
Social skills	"Let's talk about this calmly and clearly."

Tool:

Use the "Pause–Name–Connect" method:

1. Pause before reacting
2. Name what you're feeling
3. Connect with your spouse through honest dialogue

Restoration Story: From Shutdown to Connection

Marcus grew up in a home where men didn't cry, didn't talk, didn't feel. His wife, Rachel, felt alone in their marriage. After a counseling session, Marcus began naming his emotions—awkwardly at first. "I feel ashamed I didn't protect you." That moment broke years of silence. Rachel said, "That was the most intimate thing you've ever said to me." Their marriage began to heal—not through perfection, but through emotional honesty.

Emotional Honesty as Legacy

A man who cultivates emotional honesty leaves a legacy of connection. His children learn to name and navigate their emotions. His wife feels seen and safe. His ministry becomes a place of healing, not hiding.

Challenge:

What emotions have you been avoiding? What conversations have you delayed? Start today. Name it. Share it. Listen deeply. Let emotional honesty become your strength.

"Legacy-minded husbands don't just love their wives—they disciple their homes."

Reflection

PART II:

HABITS OF ACTION

CHAPTER FIVE

He Serves Without Scorekeeping

Love isn't transactional. This chapter challenges husbands to serve sacrificially, without keeping tally. Drawing from Jesus' example, it explores how acts of service—big and small—build lasting joy and mutual respect.

Real love doesn't keep a ledger. A man who serves without scorekeeping reflects the heart of Jesus, who washed feet, bore burdens, and gave Himself without demanding repayment. In marriage, this kind of love transforms homes into havens.

The Trap of Transactional Love

Scorekeeping is subtle. It sounds like:

- "I did the dishes—why haven't you thanked me?"
- "I've been patient all week—what about you?"
- "I'll give more when I get more."

But transactional love is conditional love. It turns marriage into a negotiation, not a covenant. It breeds resentment, entitlement, and emotional distance.

Illustration:

A husband once said, "I feel like I'm always giving." His wife replied, "I feel like I'm always being measured." Scorekeeping doesn't build intimacy—it builds walls.

Jesus: The Servant Who Never Kept Score

Jesus didn't serve to be noticed. He didn't tally miracles or demand reciprocity. He knelt, washed feet, healed the sick, and forgave enemies—all without keeping track.

Scripture Anchor:

"The Son of Man did not come to be served, but to serve, and to give His life as a ransom for many." —Matthew 20:28

Jesus' leadership was marked by:

- Unseen sacrifice
- Relentless compassion
- Joyful obedience
- Lavish grace

He gave—and gave again—because love is not earned. It's offered

Acts of Love: The Daily, Unseen Ministry

Love is not just spoken, it's shown. A man who serves without scorekeeping:

- Folds laundry without fanfare
- Listens without interrupting
- Carries emotional weight without complaint
- Prays for his spouse in secret
- Does the hard thing—again—because love demands it

Tool:

Create a "Service Inventory" for the week. List 5 ways you can serve your spouse without announcing it, expecting thanks, or keeping score. Then do them quietly, joyfully, and consistently.

Household Partnership: Shared Responsibility, Shared Honor

Serving isn't just romantic gestures—it is a partnership in the mundane. A servant-hearted man:

- Sees household tasks as ministry, not obligation
- Shares the load without waiting to be asked
- Honors his spouse's exhaustion with action, not advice
- Builds a culture of mutual care, not silent resentment

Challenge:

Ask your spouse: "What's one area where I can serve you more consistently?" Then do it—without reminding her you did.

Unseen Sacrifices: The Hidden Glory of Service

Some of the most powerful acts of love are never seen:

- Choosing silence over sarcasm
- Staying up late to finish what she forgot
- Giving up your preference to honor hers
- Carrying emotional burdens, she doesn't even know you're holding

These sacrifices echo the cross—where love was poured out in blood, not applause.

Illustration:

A man once said, "I realized I was waiting for a thank-you that never came. Then God whispered, 'I saw it." That moment shifted his heart from resentment to worship.

Serving as Legacy

A man who serves without scorekeeping leaves a legacy of grace. His children learn that love is not earned, it's given. His wife feels cherished, not compared. His home becomes a sanctuary, not a scoreboard.

Challenge:

Where have you been keeping score? What silent expectations have poisoned your joy? Lay them down. Serve freely. Love boldly. Model Jesus.

Closing Prayer

Lord, strip away my need to be noticed. Teach me to serve with joy, not resentment.
Help me love without keeping score, without demanding repayment, without seeking applause.
Make me a man who reflects Your servant heart—in the quiet, in the mundane, in the unseen.
In Jesus' name, Amen.

“A husband’s consistency is more romantic than any grand gesture.”

Reflection

CHAPTER SIX

He Pursues Her–Romantically and Respectfully

Romance doesn't expire with time. This chapter reignites the pursuit, offering creative ideas for date nights, exploring love languages, and respectful affection. It emphasizes that pursuit is a lifelong habit, not a honeymoon phase.

Romance isn't a phase; it's a pursuit. A man who continues to pursue his wife with intentionality and honor reflects the relentless love of Christ. Romance doesn't expire with time—it deepens with devotion.

The Myth: Romance Fades with Time

Too many marriages settle into routine and call it maturity. But routine without romance breeds emotional distance. The truth is:

- Desire doesn't die—it just gets buried under busyness
- Affection doesn't fade—it just needs fuel
- Pursuit doesn't end at the altar—it begins there

Illustration:

A wife once said, "I don't need roses—I need to know I'm still worth chasing." Romance isn't about extravagance. It's about intentionality.

Date Nights: Sacred Spaces for Connection

Date nights aren't luxuries—they're lifelines. They say, "You matter. We matter. Let's protect this."

Keys to meaningful date nights:

- Schedule them regularly—don't wait for spontaneity
- Be present—phones off, hearts open
- Try new things—adventure rekindles attraction
- Reflect and dream—talk about more than logistics

Tool:

Create a "Date Night Jar" with 20 creative ideas—some free, some adventurous, all intentional. Pull one each week and commit to it.

Love Languages: Speaking Her Heart Fluently

Every woman receives love differently. Knowing her love language is like having the key to her emotional vault.

The Five Love Languages (Gary Chapman):

Love Language	How to Pursue Her Respectfully and Romantically
Words of Affirmation	Write her notes. Speak life. Compliment sincerely.
Acts of Service	Do the task she dreads. Anticipate her needs.
Receiving Gifts	Surprise her with something meaningful—not expensive
Quality Time	Give her undivided attention. Plan intentional moments
Physical Touch	Hold her hand. Hug her often. Be tender, not rushed.

Challenge:

Ask her: "What makes you feel most loved?" Then pursue her in that language—consistently.

Intentional Affection: Daily Pursuit, Not Occasional Gesture

Affection isn't just physical, emotional, spiritual, and verbal. It's the daily pursuit that says, "I see you. I choose you. Again."

Ways to show intentional affection:

- Greet her with warmth, not distraction
- Send a midday text just to say "I'm thinking of you"
- Pray over her—out loud, with tenderness
- Compliment her character, not just her appearance
- Initiate touch with respect and sensitivity

Illustration:

One husband began kissing his wife on the forehead each morning and saying, "You're my answered prayer." That simple act reignited tenderness in their marriage.

Rekindling Desire: Passion with Honor

Desire is holy when pursued with honor. Rekindling passion means:

- Creating emotional safety
- Prioritizing her comfort and consent
- Being playful without being presumptuous
- Honoring her boundaries as sacred, not negotiable

Scripture Anchor:

"Husbands, love your wives, just as Christ loved the church and gave Himself up for her."—Ephesians 5:25

Christ's love was sacrificial, tender, and protective. So must ours be

Romance as Legacy

A man who pursues his wife romantically and respectfully leaves a legacy of love. His children learn that marriage is not a duty, it's a delight. His wife feels cherished, not tolerated. His home becomes a sanctuary of affection and honor.

Challenge:

What have you stopped doing that once made her feel pursued? Start again. Not because you have to—but because she's worth it.

Closing Prayer

Lord, teach me to pursue my wife with passion and honor.
Help me love her in ways that speak to her heart.
Rekindle desire, deepen affection, and restore joy in our marriage.
Make me a man who reflects Your relentless love—daily, tenderly, and respectfully.
In Jesus' name, Amen.

"The happiest husbands are legacy builders. They plant seeds of grace that outlive their own lifetime."

Reflection

CHAPTER SEVEN

He Speaks Blessing, Not Criticism

Words shape reality. This chapter equips husbands to speak life, affirm their wives, and replace sarcasm or silence with intentional encouragement.

A husband's words shape the emotional climate of his home. A man who speaks blessing becomes a builder of hearts, a healer of wounds, and a mirror of Christ's love. Criticism tears down—but blessing builds up.

The Damage of Sarcasm, Silence, and Criticism

Words can wound more deeply than actions. Sarcasm may sound clever, but it often masks contempt. Silence may feel safe, but it communicates indifference. Criticism may feel justified, but it erodes trust and intimacy.

Common destructive patterns:

- Sarcastic jabs disguised as humor
- Withholding affirmation as punishment
- Highlighting flaws more than celebrating strengths
- Speaking only when frustrated, not when grateful

Illustration:

A wife once said, "I'd rather hear nothing than be mocked." Her husband thought he was being funny—but she felt belittled. Sarcasm is not affection—it's erosion.

Jesus: The Voice of Blessing

Jesus never used sarcasm to correct. He spoke truth with grace, affirmation with authority, and blessing with intentionality.

Scripture Anchor:

"The tongue has the power of life and death..."—Proverbs 18:21
"Do not let any unwholesome talk come out of your mouths, but only what is helpful for building others up..."—Ephesians 4:29

Jesus spoke words that:

- Healed the broken
- Affirmed the unseen
- Restored the ashamed
- Called out destiny

Challenge:

If Jesus were speaking to your wife today, what would He say?
Speak that.

Words That Build, Affirm, and Heal

Affirmation is not flattery—it's truth spoken in love. A husband's words should be:

- **Intentional** — not reactive or careless
- **Specific** — not vague or generic
- **Consistent** — not occasional or conditional
- **Life-giving** — not draining or dismissive

Examples of affirming words:

- "I'm proud of how you handled that."
- "You're beautiful—inside and out."
- "I see how hard you're working, and I'm grateful."
- "You make this house feel like home."
- "I trust your wisdom."

Tool:

Create a "Blessing Journal." Each day, write one sentence of affirmation about your wife. Share it with her weekly—or leave notes where she'll find them.

Replacing Criticism with Encouragement

Step-by-step transformation:

1. **Catch the impulse.** When tempted to criticize, pause and ask: "Is this helpful or hurtful?"
2. **Redirect the tone.** Replace sarcasm with sincerity.
3. **Speak life in conflict.** Even in disagreement, affirm her value.
4. **Practice daily encouragement.** Make it a habit, not a holiday.

Illustration:

One husband began texting his wife a blessing every morning. "You're my favorite person." "You're wise and strong." Over time, their communication shifted from tension to tenderness.

Speaking Blessing as Legacy

A man who speaks blessings leaves a legacy of love. His children learn how to honor. His wife feels safe, seen, and celebrated. His home becomes a sanctuary of grace.

Challenge:

Audit your words this week. Are they building or breaking? Replace one sarcastic comment with a sincere compliment. Replace one moment of silence with a spoken blessing.

Closing Prayer

Lord, teach me to speak life.
Strip sarcasm from my tongue and criticism from my heart.
Fill my mouth with words that build, affirm, and heal.
Help me bless my wife daily—with truth, tenderness, and intentional love.
Make me a man whose words reflect Your heart.
In Jesus' name, Amen.

"A happy husband doesn't just protect his home—he cultivates peace within it."

Reflection

CHAPTER EIGHT

He Invests in Shared Dreams

Marriage thrives on shared purpose. This chapter guides couples in vision casting, goal setting, and dreaming together. It shows how aligning on mission strengthens unity and gives meaning to the mundane.

Marriage is not just about companionship—it's about co-mission. When a husband invests in shared dreams, he becomes a visionary partner, not just a passive participant. Shared purpose is the soil where intimacy flourishes.

The Power of Shared Purpose

Couples who dream together, grow together. When a husband and wife align their hearts around a common vision, they move from survival to significance.

Without shared purpose, marriage can drift into:

- Parallel lives with little emotional connection
- Conflicting priorities and unmet expectations
- A lack of excitement or forward momentum

With shared purpose, marriage becomes:

- A partnership of passion and direction
- A safe space for dreaming and daring
- A legacy-building union that blesses others

Scripture Anchor:

"Can two walk together unless they are agreed?"—Amos 3:3
"Write the vision and make it plain..."—Habakkuk 2:2

Vision Casting as a Couple

A husband who invests in shared dreams doesn't just ask, "What do I want?" He asks, "What do we want to build together?"

Vision casting includes:

- **Spiritual goals** — growing in faith, serving together
- **Relational goals** — cultivating emotional intimacy
- **Family goals** — parenting, legacy, traditions
- **Financial goals** — stewardship, generosity, security
- **Missional goals** — how your marriage blesses others

Tool:

Schedule a "Vision Retreat." Take one weekend a year to pray, dream, and plan together. Use guided questions like:

- **What do we feel called to in this season?**
- **What legacy do we want to leave?**
- **What are our top three goals for the next year?**

🛠 Goal Setting That Strengthens Intimacy

Dreams without action become frustration. A husband who invests in shared dreams helps turn vision into movement.

Healthy goal setting includes:

- **Mutual input** — both voices matter
- **Realistic timelines** — pace with grace
- **Celebration of progress** — honor the journey
- **Adaptability** — dreams evolve, and that's okay

Example:

Instead of saying, "We should save more," say, "Let's set a goal to save $5,000 this year toward our dream home—and celebrate each milestone."

Intimacy grows when:

- You dream aloud together

- You solve problems as a team
- You celebrate wins, not just endure losses

Shared Mission Deepens Emotional Connection

When couples serve a greater purpose together, their hearts knit more tightly. Shared mission creates shared meaning.

Ways to live on mission together:

- Host a small group or Bible study
- Volunteer in your community
- Mentor younger couples
- Create resources that bless others
- Support each other's callings with joy, not jealousy

Illustration:

One couple began leading marriage workshops together. Their shared mission not only helped others, but it reignited their own passion and unity.

From Me to We: A Shift in Mindset

A husband who invests in shared dreams moves from "my goals" to "our calling." He listens, collaborates, and champions his wife's dreams as much as his own.

Questions to ask regularly:

- "What's stirring in your heart lately?"
- "What dream of yours can I support this month?"
- "How can we align our calendars with our calling?"

Challenge:

Make a "Dream Board" together. Include spiritual, relational, financial, and missional goals. Place it somewhere visible. Pray over it weekly.

Closing Prayer

Lord, make me a husband who dreams with my wife. Help us cast vision, set goals, and walk in unity. Let our marriage reflect Your purpose and passion. Teach me to listen, support, and lead with humility. May our shared mission deepen our intimacy and bless others.
In Jesus' name, Amen.

"Spiritual intimacy begins when a husband prays not just for his wife, but with her."

Reflection

CHAPTER NINE

He Protects Her Peace

A husband can be a shield or a storm. This chapter explores how to guard the emotional, spiritual, and physical peace of the home. It includes strategies for managing stress, setting boundaries, and creating a sanctuary of rest.

A godly husband is not just a provider—he is a protector of peace. He stands watch over the emotional climate of his home, shields his wife from unnecessary stress, and cultivates a sanctuary where rest, safety, and spiritual renewal flourish.

The Threats to Peace

Peace is fragile. It's constantly under assault—from external pressures, internal conflicts, and spiritual warfare. A husband who fails to guard peace allows chaos to creep in.

Common threats to peace:

- Unchecked stress and busyness
- Emotional volatility or unresolved conflict
- Financial strain and poor communication
- Spiritual apathy or compromise
- Toxic relationships or lack of boundaries

Scripture Anchor:

"The Lord bless you and keep you; the Lord make His face shine on you and be gracious to you; the Lord turn His face toward you and give you peace."—Numbers 6:24–26
"Let the peace of Christ rule in your hearts..."—Colossians 3:15

Emotional Peace: Guarding Her Heart

A husband protects emotional peace by being emotionally present, safe, and steady. He listens without fixing, affirms without judgment, and creates space for vulnerability.

Strategies for emotional protection:

- Be a calming presence. Don't escalate tension—diffuse it.
- Validate her emotions. Don't dismiss or minimize.
- Create rhythms of connection. Weekly check-ins, date nights, prayer together.
- Avoid emotional withdrawal. Silence can feel like abandonment.

Challenge:

Ask her, "What's weighing on you this week?" Then listen—without interrupting, defending, or solving.

Spiritual Peace: Guarding the Atmosphere

A husband is the spiritual gatekeeper of his home. He discerns what enters, what influences, and what lingers. He leads in prayer, worship, and spiritual warfare.

Strategies for spiritual protection:

- Pray over your wife daily. Out loud, with authority and tenderness.
- Anoint your home. Declare it a place of peace and protection.
- Guard against spiritual compromise. What you allow in (media, attitudes, habits) affects the atmosphere.
- Lead in spiritual rhythms. Devotions, Sabbath rest, worship.

Illustration:

One husband began praying over each room in his house every morning. His wife said, "I feel safer when you pray." Peace isn't passive, it's pursued.

Physical Peace: Creating a Sanctuary

The home should be a refuge, not a battleground. A husband protects physical peace by managing stress, setting boundaries, and cultivating rest.

Strategies for physical protection:

- Manage your own stress. Don't bring chaos home.
- Set boundaries with work, technology, and toxic people.
- Create spaces of rest. Declutter, light candles, and play worship music.
- Honor Sabbath rhythms. Rest is holy—and healing.

Tool:

Design a "Peace Plan" for your home. Include:

- Quiet hours
- No-phone zones
- Weekly rest rituals
- Conflict resolution guideline

Guarding Against Chaos and Spiritual Attack

Peace must be defended. The enemy seeks to divide, distract, and destroy. A husband must be spiritually alert and emotionally mature.

Signs of spiritual attack:

- Sudden conflict or confusion
- Emotional heaviness or despair
- Disunity and miscommunication
- Loss of joy or spiritual hunger

Response:

- Pray with authority. Rebuke chaos, invite peace.
- Fast and intercede. Stand in the gap.
- Speak Scripture aloud. Declare truth over your home.
- Invite accountability. Don't fight alone.

Scripture Anchor:

"The thief comes only to steal and kill and destroy; I have come that they may have life, and have it to the full." —John 10:10

Peace as Intimacy Builder

When a wife feels safe—emotionally, spiritually, and physically—intimacy deepens. Peace is the soil where trust grows.

Peace cultivates:

- Emotional openness
- Spiritual unity
- Physical affection
- Relational joy

Challenge:

Ask her: "What makes you feel most at peace in our home?" Then build that—together.

Closing Prayer

Lord, make me a guardian of peace.
Teach me to protect my wife's heart, mind, and spirit.
Let our home be a sanctuary of rest, not a source of stress.
Help me lead with gentleness, pray with authority, and love with consistency.
I rebuke chaos, confusion, and spiritual attack—and I declare peace over our marriage.
In Jesus' name, Amen.

*"When a husband honors his wife's voice,
he amplifies the harmony of their home."*

Reflection

CHAPTER TEN

He Laughs Often and Lightens the Load

Laughter is holy. This chapter celebrates humor, playfulness, and joy as spiritual practices. It encourages husbands to be a source of levity, helping their wives carry life's burdens with grace and grit.

A godly husband doesn't just carry burdens—he lightens them. He brings laughter into heaviness, joy into the grind, and playfulness into the pressure. His presence becomes a refuge, his humor a healing balm, and his joy a spiritual weapon.

The Weight of Life—and the Gift of Levity

Life is heavy. Bills, deadlines, parenting, ministry, conflict, grief—it all piles up. But laughter is God's gift to help us breathe again.

Without joy, marriage can become:

- A business partnership instead of a love story
- A survival strategy instead of a sanctuary
- A place of tension instead of tenderness

With joy, marriage becomes:

- A safe space for emotional release
- A rhythm of celebration in the mundane
- A reminder that love is not just serious—it's sacred and silly

Scripture Anchor:

"A cheerful heart is good medicine, but a crushed spirit dries up the bones." —Proverbs 17:22

"The joy of the Lord is your strength."—Nehemiah 8:10

Humor and Playfulness as Spiritual Practices

Joy is not optional—it's essential. It's a fruit of the Spirit, a mark of maturity, and a weapon against despair.

Spiritual benefits of laughter:

- Releases emotional tension
- Builds relational intimacy
- Disarms conflict and defensiveness
- Invites the presence of God into everyday life

Jesus modeled joy:

He welcomed children, told stories with wit, and celebrated at weddings. His joy was magnetic, not manufactured.

A Husband Who Lightens the Load

A husband who laughs often doesn't ignore reality—he infuses it with hope. He helps his wife carry life's burdens with grace and grit.

Ways to lighten the load:

- **Use humor to defuse tension.** A well-timed joke can soften a hard moment.
- **Be playful in the mundane.** Dance in the kitchen. Sing in the car. Make her laugh on laundry day.
- **Celebrate small wins.** Don't wait for anniversaries—celebrate Tuesday.
- **Be emotionally available.** Sometimes, lightening the load means listening deeply, then offering joy.

Illustration:

One husband started a tradition: every Friday, he'd leave a silly note in his wife's purse. "You're my favorite human." "You survived Monday—here's your trophy." Over time, those notes became sacred reminders of joy in the grind.

Practical Joy-Building Strategies

1. Create a "Joy Ritual"

Start each day with something light—prayer, laughter, music, a shared moment.

2. Plan Playful Dates

Not just dinner—go bowling, play mini golf, take a cooking class, build a blanket fort.

3. Laugh at Yourself

Model humility and humor. Don't take yourself too seriously.

4. Invite Joy into Conflict

After resolving tension, say: "Let's laugh again." Watch a funny video. Share a memory. Reconnect.

5. Protect Joy from Stress

Set boundaries with work, media, and negativity. Guard your home's emotional climate.

Joy as Intimacy Builder

Laughter builds trust. Playfulness opens hearts. Joy makes space for vulnerability.

Joy cultivates:

- Emotional safety
- Relational resilience
- Physical affection
- Spiritual unity

Challenge:

Ask your wife: "What makes you laugh?" Then do more of that. Be her joy-bringer, not just her burden-sharer.

Closing Prayer

Lord, teach me to laugh often and love deeply.
Help me bring joy into our home, levity into our stress, and playfulness into our routines.
Make me a husband who lightens the load—not just with strength, but with gladness.
Let my laughter be holy, my humor healing, and my joy contagious.
In Jesus' name, Amen.

"Joy is a discipline, not a mood.
Happy husbands choose it daily."

Reflection

PART III:

HABITS OF GROWTH

CHAPTER ELEVEN

He Learns Continuously

The Teachable Spirit That Transforms a Marriage

A man who stops learning stops leading. A husband who refuses to grow quietly forfeits the influence God designed him to carry. But a man who learns continuously—who humbles himself to receive wisdom, correction, and insight—becomes a wellspring of strength, stability, and spiritual vitality in his home.

The Beauty of a Teachable Spirit

There is something undeniably attractive about a teachable man. Not just to his wife, but to his children, his community, and even to God. Scripture says, *"The wise listen and add to their learning"* (Proverbs 1:5). A teachable spirit is not weakness; it's wisdom wrapped in humility. It's the posture of a man who knows that love requires listening, and leadership demands learning.

In marriage, a teachable spirit says:

- "I don't have all the answers, but I'm committed to finding them."
- "I'm willing to grow, even when it's uncomfortable."
- "I value your voice, and I'm open to change."

This kind of man doesn't just win arguments—he wins hearts.

Learning as an Act of Love

Too often, learning is framed as academic or optional. But in marriage, learning is an act of love.

When a husband studies his wife's heart, reads books to understand her needs better, seeks mentors to sharpen his character, or attends enrichment events to deepen their bond—he is saying, "You matter enough for me to grow."

Learning becomes a form of pursuit.
It's how a man says, "I'm still chasing you," even after years of marriage.
It's how he says, "I want to be better—for you, for us, for God."

Growth Through Books, Mentors, and Marriage Enrichment

A man who learns continuously builds a toolbox of wisdom. He doesn't wait for a crisis to seek counsel—he pursues growth proactively.

Here are three powerful pathways:

- **Books**: Reading is not just for scholars—it's for husbands who want to lead with insight. Whether it's a book on communication, conflict resolution, or spiritual intimacy, each page can become a stepping stone toward a more profound connection.
- **Mentors**: Every man needs a Paul, a Barnabas, and a Timothy. A mentor to guide him, a peer to walk with him, and someone younger to pour into. Mentorship accelerates growth and anchors a man in accountability.
- **Marriage Enrichment**: Retreats, workshops, and counseling are not signs of weakness—they're signs of wisdom. Investing in your marriage is like tending to a garden: the more intentional the care, the more abundant the fruit.

Lifelong Learning as Leadership

Leadership in marriage is not domination—it's devotion.
And devotion requires development.

When a husband commits to lifelong learning, he models humility, resilience, and spiritual maturity. He becomes a thermostat, not a thermometer—setting the climate of growth in his home rather than reacting to it.

He learns continuously because:

- His love is active, not passive.
- His leadership is servant-hearted, not self-centered.
- His legacy is built one lesson at a time.

A Prayer for the Teachable Husband

Lord, make me a man who learns with joy and listens with grace. Give me the humility to receive correction, the courage to pursue growth, and the wisdom to lead through love. May my teachable spirit reflect Your heart, and may my learning become a gift to my wife, my family, and the world You've called me to serve. Amen.

"Marriage is a ministry. A happy husband treats his vows like a calling, not a contract."

Reflection

CHAPTER TWELVE

He Builds Brotherhood

Why No Man Thrives Alone

Isolation is not just lonely—it's lethal. It dulls discernment, weakens resolve, and leaves a man vulnerable to temptation, discouragement, and spiritual drift. God never designed men to walk alone. From Eden to the early church, brotherhood has been a sacred strategy for strength, growth, and protection.

A man who builds brotherhood builds a shield around his soul.

The Danger of Isolation

The enemy loves a lone wolf.
When a man withdraws—emotionally, spiritually, relationally—he becomes easy prey. Scripture warns, *"Whoever isolates himself seeks his own desire; he breaks out against all sound judgment"* (Proverbs 18:1). Isolation breeds deception. It convinces a man that he's fine when he's floundering, strong when he's slipping, and wise when he's wandering.

Isolation whispers:

- "No one understands."
- "You're better off handling this alone."
- "If they knew the real you, they'd walk away."

But brotherhood shouts back:

- "You're not alone."
- "We've got your back."
- "Let's walk through this together."

The Power of Male Friendships

Healthy male friendships are not optional—they're essential. They offer laughter, challenge, truth, and grace. They sharpen a man's character and soften his heart. They remind him that strength is found in shared struggle, not solo survival.

A true brother:

- Celebrates another's wins without envy.
- Confronts your sin without shame.
- Covers your weakness with prayer and presence.

These friendships don't just happen—they're built. Brick by brick. Conversation by conversation. Vulnerability by vulnerability.

Models of Brotherhood in Scripture

God gives us vivid pictures of brotherhood throughout Scripture:

- **David and Jonathan**: A covenant friendship marked by loyalty, sacrifice, and spiritual alignment.
- **Jesus and the Twelve**: A band of brothers shaped by mission, mentorship, and mutual transformation.
- **Paul and Timothy**: A spiritual father-son relationship rooted in encouragement, instruction, and legacy.

These models remind us: brotherhood is not just about hanging out—it's about holding each other up.

Building Brotherhood Today

Here are practical ways to cultivate healthy brotherhood:

- **Join a Men's Group**: Whether through church, community, or online platforms, consistent connection with other men fosters growth and accountability.
- **Pursue One-on-One Discipleship**: Find a mentor or become one. Spiritual counsel deepens wisdom and strengthens resolve.

- **Create a Circle of Accountability**: Invite 2–3 trusted brothers to ask the hard questions, pray regularly, and speak truth in love.
- **Show Up Consistently**: Brotherhood is built through presence. Be the man who shows up—at the hospital, the funeral, the celebration, and the struggle.

The Pitfalls of Going It Alone

Men who go it alone often fall into:

- **Moral compromise**: No one to challenge or correct.
- **Emotional numbness**: No one to process pain or celebrate joy.
- **Spiritual stagnation**: No one to stir hunger or offer counsel.

The cost of isolation is too high.
The reward of brotherhood is too rich.

A Prayer for Brotherhood

Lord, surround me with brothers who sharpen, strengthen, and speak truth. Give me the courage to pursue connection, the humility to receive counsel, and the grace to offer friendship. Break every lie of isolation and build in me a heart that values brotherhood as a gift from You. May my life be marked by loyalty, love, and shared pursuit of Your Kingdom, Amen.

Reflection

CHAPTER THIRTEEN

He Owns His Mistakes and Grows from Them

Failure Isn't Fatal—It's Formative

Every man stumbles.

But not every man stands back up, learns, and leads with greater wisdom.

The difference isn't perfection—it's humility.

A husband who owns his mistakes becomes a man God can mold, a leader his wife can trust, and a father his children can follow.

The Lie of Shame

Shame says, "You blew it—now bury it."

But grace says, "You blew it—now build from it."

Too many husbands live haunted by past failures:

- Harsh words that wounded
- Decisions that divided
- Moments of weakness that betrayed trust

But failure is not the end—it's the invitation. To repent. To repair. To grow.

Scripture reminds us, *"Though the righteous fall seven times, they rise again"* (Proverbs 24:16). Rising begins with owning.

The Path of Repentance

Repentance is not just an apology—it's a transformation.
It's a turning of heart, a change of direction, and a commitment to do differently.

A husband who repents:

- Names the wrong without excuses.
- Seeks forgiveness without manipulation.
- Makes amends without delay.

Repentance is not weakness—it's spiritual strength.
It's the doorway to healing and the foundation for trust.

Stories of Transformation

Marcus, a husband who once led with pride, found himself estranged from his wife after years of emotional neglect. One night, broken and alone, he cried out to God—not for rescue, but for renewal. He began counseling, joined a men's group, and wrote a letter of confession to his wife. That letter became the first brick in rebuilding their marriage.

Keith, a father who struggled with anger, once terrified his children with outbursts. After a painful confrontation with his teenage son, he chose to own it. He asked for forgiveness, installed accountability software, and began weekly check-ins with a mentor. Today, his home is marked by peace, not fear.

These men didn't just say "I'm sorry." On the contrary, they said, "I'm changing."

Tools for Resilient Growth

Here are practical tools for husbands who want to grow through failure:

- **The Mirror Moment**: Take time weekly to reflect—What did I say or do that missed the mark? What triggered it? What truth do I need to embrace?

- **The Confession Habit**: Normalize saying "I was wrong." Practice it with your wife, children, and friends. It builds trust, demonstrates maturity, and models it.
- **The Growth Journal**: Track lessons learned from mistakes. Write down what happened, what you felt, what you learned, and what you'll do differently.
- **The Accountability Circle:** Invite 2–3 men to walk with you. Share your struggles, receive counsel, and celebrate progress.

Growth is not automatic. No, it is intentional. And it begins with *humility*.

The Fruit of Humility

When a husband owns his mistakes:

- His wife feels safe.
- His children feel seen.
- His home becomes a place of grace.

Humility doesn't make a man weak—it makes him wise. Most importantly, it opens the door to intimacy, integrity, and influence.

A Prayer for Growth

Lord, give me the courage to face my failures,
the humility to own them,
and the wisdom to grow through them.
Teach me to repent quickly, repair gently, and lead graciously.
May my mistakes become milestones of maturity,
and may my life reflect Your redemptive power.
Amen.

"A happy husband doesn't chase perfection—he cultivates presence. Joy begins when we show up fully, not flawlessly."

Reflection

CHAPTER FOURTEEN

He Honors Her Story

Empathy as a Spiritual Discipline

Every woman carries a story.
Not just a timeline of events—but a tapestry of dreams, disappointments, victories, and wounds.
To love her well, a husband must learn her story—not just the facts, but the feelings. Not just the chapters, but the undercurrents.

A man who honors his wife's story becomes a safe place for her soul.

Her Story Is Sacred...

Your wife is not just your partner—she is a daughter of God, shaped by experiences that preceded you and dreams that extend beyond you.
Her story includes:

- Childhood memories that shaped her identity.
- Past relationships that left marks—some beautiful, some bruising.
- Hopes she's whispered to God in the quiet.
- Fears she's never spoken aloud.

To honor her story is to say: "I see you. I value you. I want to know you—not just what you do, but who you are."

Scripture calls husbands to *"live with your wives in an understanding way"* (1 Peter 3:7).
Understanding begins with listening. Honor begins with empathy.

The Discipline of Empathy

Empathy is not a personality trait—it's a spiritual discipline.
It requires:

- **Presence:** Being fully there, without distraction or agenda.
- **Curiosity:** Asking questions that invite depth, not just detail.
- **Compassion:** Feeling with her, not just for her.

Empathy says:

- "Tell me more."
- "That must have been hard."
- "I'm here with you."

It's not about fixing, but it is about feeling.
It's not about solving, but it is about seeing.

Honoring Her Voice

Many wives feel unheard—not because their husbands are silent, but because they're not truly listening.
To honor her voice means:

- Letting her speak without interruption.
- Validating her emotions without defensiveness.
- Welcoming her perspective without minimizing.

When a husband honors his wife's voice, he communicates:
"You matter. Your thoughts matter. Your feelings matter."

This creates emotional safety—the soil where intimacy grows.

Healing Through Connection

When a wife feels known, she begins to heal.
When she feels honored, she begins to trust.
When she feels safe, she begins to flourish.

Empathy becomes the bridge between her past and your shared future. It transforms marriage from coexistence to communion.

Case Study: Elijah and Stephanie

Stephanie carried deep wounds from childhood abandonment. For years, Elijah tried to "fix" her pain with advice and Scripture. But one day, he simply sat with her, held her hand, and said, "I want to understand your story. I want to feel what you felt." That moment changed everything.

Stephanie didn't need a solution, she needed solidarity. Elijah's empathy became the beginning of her healing.

Practical Ways to Honor Her Story

- **Create a Story Night**: Set aside time to ask about her childhood, her dreams, her fears. Listen without judgment.
- **Keep a Wife Journal**: Record things she shares—what matters to her, what hurts, what brings joy. Use it to pray and pursue her heart.
- **Ask Intentional Questions**: "What's something you wish I understood better?" "What's a dream you've put on hold?" "What's a memory that shaped you?"
- **Practice Reflective Listening**: Repeat back what she says to show you're truly hearing her. "So what I hear you saying is…"

The Fruit of Honor

When a husband honors his wife's story:

- She feels cherished, not just chosen.
- She feels understood, not just accommodated.
- She feels loved, not just married.

Honor is not just romance; it's reverence. It's treating her story as holy ground.

A Prayer for Empath

Lord, teach me to listen with my heart, to see beyond the surface, and to honor the sacred story You've written in my wife. Help me to be a safe place for her soul, a student of her heart,

and a partner in her healing. May empathy become my daily discipline, and may our marriage reflect Your tender love. Amen.

"A husband's humility is the soil where intimacy grows."

Reflection

CHAPTER FIFTEEN

He Lives with Legacy in Mind

Marriage Is Generational

Some men live for the moment.
Wise men live for the generations.
A husband who lives with legacy in mind doesn't just love his wife for today—he builds a marriage that echoes into eternity.

Marriage is not just a private covenant.
It's a generational calling.
It shapes children, influences communities, and leaves fingerprints on the future.

Legacy Begins with Vision

Legacy is not about wealth or reputation, it's about impact.
It's the spiritual, emotional, and relational inheritance you leave behind.

Ask yourself:

- What will my children say about how I loved their mother?
- What will my grandchildren learn from the way we resolve conflict?
- What will my marriage model to young couples watching from afar?

Legacy begins when a man lifts his eyes from the moment and sees the ripple effect of his choices.

Scripture says, *"A good man leaves an inheritance to his children's children"*

(Proverbs 13:22).
That inheritance includes wisdom, witness, and love.

Fathering with Eternity in Mind

Your marriage is your children's first theology lesson.
They learn about grace, forgiveness, sacrifice, and covenant by watching how you treat their mother.

To father well:

- Speak words that bless, not bruise.
- Model humility, not hypocrisy.
- Show consistency, not convenience.

Your children will remember:

- How you prayed together.
- How you handled pressure.
- How you honored your wife when no one was watching.

You're not just raising kids, but you are raising future husbands, wives, and leaders.
Father with eternity in mind.

Marriage as a Mirror of Heaven

Marriage is not just temporal—it's theological.
It reflects Christ and the Church.
It's a living parable of covenant love, sacrificial grace, and eternal union.

When husbands love with legacy in mind:

- They forgive quickly.
- They serve sacrificially.
- They pursue intimacy with intentionality.

Your marriage becomes a sanctuary—where heaven touches earth.

The Cost of Living Small

Men who live only for the moment:

- Chase comfort over calling.
- Choose silence over spiritual leadership.
- Settle for survival instead of significance.

But legacy-minded husbands:

- Invest in what lasts.
- Speak life into future generations.
- Build altars, not just routines.

Don't just aim for longevity—aim for legacy.
Longevity lasts a lifetime.
Legacy lasts forever.

Building a Legacy Marriage

Here are practical ways to live with legacy in mind:

- **Write a Family Blessing**: Craft a prayer or declaration that speaks life over your wife, children, and future generations.
- **Create a Marriage Mission Statement**: Define the purpose, values, and vision of your union. Revisit it annually.
- **Establish Traditions of Faith**: Weekly prayer nights, annual retreats, or legacy letters—rituals that root your family in God's story.
- **Mentor Younger Couples**: Share your journey. Your scars and victories can guide others toward health and holiness.

The Fruit of Legacy

When a husband lives with legacy in mind:

- His wife feels secure in his vision.
- His children walk in the shadow of his faith.
- His home becomes a lighthouse for generations.

Legacy is not built in a day. No, it is built daily.
Through small choices, sacred rhythms, and surrendered love.

A Prayer for Legacy

Lord, help me to live beyond the moment. Give me vision for generations, wisdom for fathering,
and grace for loving my wife with eternity in view. May my marriage reflect Your covenant,
and may my life leave a legacy of faith, hope, and love. Let my home be a holy echo of heaven,
Amen.

"The happiest husbands are legacy builders. They plant seeds of grace that outlive their own lifetime."

Reflection

Conclusion

Becoming the Husband She Always Prayed For

Progress. Presence. Purpose.

You don't have to be perfect.
You just have to be present.
You don't need every answer.
You just need a willing heart.

If you've made it this far, it means you care.
You want to grow.
You want to love well.
You want to become the husband your wife prayed for—whether she's beside you now, waiting for you in faith, or watching from heaven.

This journey is not about performance; it's about transformation.
It's not about checking boxes, it's about changing hearts.
And it begins, repeatedly, with grace.

A Word of Encouragement

Brother, you are not alone.
Every man who chooses to love sacrificially, lead humbly, and grow intentionally walks this road with you. There will be setbacks. There will be moments of doubt. But there will also be breakthroughs, healing, laughter, and a legacy. Your wife doesn't need a flawless man. She needs a faithful one. One who listens. One who learns. One who leans on God. You are becoming that man: one prayer, one choice, one chapter at a time.

A Prayer of Commitment

Lord, I surrender my pride, my past, and my plans.
Make me the husband you've called me to be.
Teach me to love with patience, lead with humility, and serve with joy.
Help me to honor my wife's story, protect her heart, and pursue her daily.
May my marriage reflect Your grace, and may my life leave a legacy of faith.
I commit to progress, not perfection—to presence, not performance—to purpose, not passivity.
In Jesus' name, Amen.

Reflection Questions

Take time to reflect, journal, or discuss with a trusted brother:

1. What chapter challenged me the most—and why?
2. Where have I grown in my understanding of love and leadership?
3. What habits or attitudes do I need to surrender to God?
4. How can I better honor my wife's voice, story, and dreams?
5. What legacy do I want my marriage to leave behind?
6. Who can walk with me in accountability and encouragement?

An Invitation to Keep Walking

This book is not the finish line. No, it is a launching pad.
Keep walking.
Keep praying.
Keep showing up.

Let grace be your fuel.
Let Scripture be your compass.
Let love be your legacy.

You are becoming the husband she prayed for.
Not because you're perfect—but because you're present.
Not because you've arrived—but because you're committed to the journey.

And that, brother, is the kind of man heaven celebrates.

Marriage is not a destination—it's a sacred journey of becoming. The *15 Habits* outlined in this book are not just behavioral tweaks or clever strategies. They are soul-deep commitments to love with intention, lead with humility, and live with joy. They are the daily choices that transform a man into the kind of husband who doesn't just survive marriage but sanctifies it.

A happy husband has not mastered perfection, but one who has embraced pursuit—pursuit of his wife's heart, pursuit of God's presence, and pursuit of the kind of legacy that echoes through generations. Joy is cultivated, intimacy is nurtured, and spiritual strength is forged in the quiet, consistent moments of obedience and grace.

So now, the question is not "What kind of marriage do you have?" but "What kind of man are you becoming?"

Let these habits become holy rhythms. Let your love be loud, your prayers be fierce, and your presence be healing. And when your wife looks at you—whether in the fire of conflict or the warmth of laughter—may she see a man who is not just happy, but holy. Not just strong but surrendered. Not just married, but deeply, joyfully, and faithfully hers.

Your journey doesn't end here. It begins anew—every morning, every moment, every choice. *Go now and live it well!*

Reflection

www.ingramcontent.com/pod-product-compliance
Lightning Source LLC
Chambersburg PA
CBHW031438270326
41930CB00007B/759

* 9 7 8 1 9 5 3 6 7 1 1 2 7 *